Introduction

The visitor, arriving either from Europe or any other countries besides Europe, is amazed by the outstanding geographical potentialities of Budapest. The romantic Buda hills, the plain of Pest and the Danube with its shiny water, which divides the former separate towns Buda and Pest, give a special atmosphere to the town. It is gorgeous to see the murmuring metropolis or its lights at night from the top of one of the Buda hills. And if after this perspective view we make a more detailed examination of the town, wander about the streets or enter some museums, we can learn a many-thousand-year-old history rich in events. People already lived in the territory of the actual town in the primitive age. Archaeologists excavated settlements of different cultures from the stone, bronze, and the iron age. (The exciting material of finds can be seen at the National Museum.) The great invasions BC brought Scythian and Celtic tribes to the area, which were followed by the Romans in the first century. The Roman legions

occupied the western part of today's Hungary, which under the name of Pannonia Province became part of the largest empire in the ancient times. Aquincum was the capital of the Eastern part of the Province (Lower Pannonia). The ruins of the former (2nd and 4th century) flourishing town can be found often in very good conditions at several places in Óbuda. The Romans were followed by the Huns eager to fight. According to the medieval legends the town was named after Attila's brother, Buda. The invasion sent newer and newer people to the territory. Goths, Longobards then Avars settled here. The empire of the Avars was destroyed by Charlemagne, the Frank king. (This usually bloody change of peoples can also be seen among the archaeological finds of the National Museum.) The Magyars appeared in the Carpathian basin in the late ninth century under the leadership of Árpád and Kurszán. The reining tribes settled in the territory of today's Budapest. The rulers of the Árpád dynasty first did not make Buda the centre of the country, but Székesfehérvár and Esztergom. In spite of that Buda and Pest started developing slowly, which was stopped by the ravages of the Mongols in 1241. After the Mongol invasion though, king Béla IV had a fortress built in Buda to defend the area. The town slowly grew to be strong and became the royal residence by the end of the 14th century. Sigismund of Luxembourg (Hungarian king and then German emperor) had a beautiful Gothic palace built on the castle hill, which was developed by king Matthias, the internationally well-known, Renaissance ruler. Buda turned into a real Renaissance town with buildings, institutions, industry and

trade of European standard in the 15th century. Its prominent function had also a great influence on the development of Pest, lying on the other bank of the River Danube. Pest grew into an important industrial and trade centre. Only the development of Óbuda, built on the Roman heritage, remained behind. The flourishing 15th century was followed by a less successful age. The Turks occupied almost one-third of the country and Buda as well in 1541. The Turkish rule did not destroy the town during 150 years, in fact several Turkish buildings, mosques, baths and houses of Eastern character appeared besides the former buildings of Gothic or Renaissance style. Some of these can be seen even today in their glory (Király bath, Gül Baba's tomb). The decay of Buda happened in 1686, when the united Christian troops reoccupied the town. After the long siege and the following senseless massacre almost all the buildings were destroyed, and hardly any people survived. After the Turkish rule the Habsburg dynasty succeeded to the Hungarian throne. During the Habsburg empire Buda lost its outstanding role. It had minor importance in

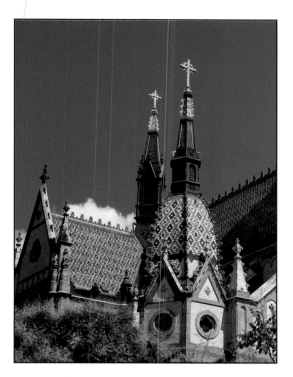

the country until the 19th century. From that time though Buda as well as Pest started to be more and more important. The aristocracy, nobility and citizens fired by national feelings turned the towns into the centres of the Hungarian culture and economy. Beautiful palaces and buildings were built. Buda and Pest started to become similar to the towns of European standards. Finally the revolution of 1848 made it possible for Buda and Pest to become the centres of political life, too. Nothing could stop their development now. Their flourishing continued after the suppression of the revolution during the years of absolutism, while in

fact they started to improve as never seen before after the Compromise of 1867. One of the most important events in the history of the town is when at last Buda, Pest and Óbuda were united in 1872. The new town grew into a real metropolis by the turn of the century. Budapest (mainly Pest lying on the left bank of the river) became the centre of business life in the country. Many boulevards, palaces, were built. Theatres, schools, banks, offices grew up almost from the nothing. Infrastructure, public transport, drainage, street lighting developed very quickly. An underground system was built for the first time on the continent in 1896. The World Expo took place in Hungary in 1896 on the occasion of the l000th anniversary of the settlement of the Magyars as an appreciation of the fantastic economic development. Great figures of Hungarian architecture designed new buildings in the town (József Hild, Miklós Ybl, Mihály Pollack, Frigyes Feszl, Imre Steindl, Ödön Lechner, etc.). The quick progress of Budapest was held back by the First World War, then during the Second World War the town was ruined again. The Germans blew up all the

bridges over the Danube while escaping, and almost every important building got damaged in the battle. The citizens of Budapest rebuilt the town in 1945, and they had to do it again in 1956, when Russian tanks destroyed everything. Budapest has been devastated through its history many times, though it has always been able to renew and preserve its own metropolitan but still familiar atmosphere. If you want to wander about in this town, you can go on a real historical tour. From the ancient ruins of Aquincum, through the houses in Gothic and Renaissance style up in the castle district, to the Neorenaissance or Art Nouveau palaces and buildings of Pest, you can find all styles of architecture. While having a look at the buildings of old times you can get to know the histori-

cal events, which although threw difficulties in the way but could not stop the development of the town. Nowadays Budapest can be said without exaggeration to be the capital of not only Hungary but of Middle Europe and one of the most important cultural centres of the continent. The intellectual life of the city was formed by outstanding figures of world culture. Several distinguished musicians lived here such as Ferenc Liszt, Béla Bartók, Ferenc Lehár, Zoltán Kodály or the Austrian composer Gustav Mahler, as well as some of the masters of fine arts of international fame in the 20th century, for example László Moholy-Nagy and Lajos Kassák. Alexander Korda made his first films here. Various great scientists of our century pursued their studies here such as János Neuman, Sándor Ferenczi, Albert Szent-Györgyi or Károly Polányi. The progress of Budapest had a greater dynamism in the last decade. Numerous concerts, theatre performances and places to have fun await their visitors. It is easy to spend a few days or even weeks here and if you feel the city's particular romantic style and atmosphere or if you taste the vivid life of Budapest a little, you will surely return.

The Castle Hill and the Castle District

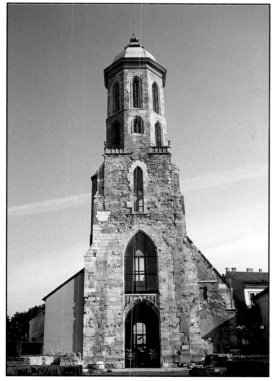

The Castle Hill of Buda is one-and-half kilometer long, half kilometer wide on the widest point, and raises 180 meters above sea level. Using the good aptitude of the area, the place has been inhabited from the most ancient ages, on the slopes of the Castle Hill. A larger settlement was formed in the 13th century, when King Béla IV ordered to construct a castle here after the invasion of the Tatars; he put his throne here. The goal of the urbanisation was rather strategic, but also had tactical reasons. The reason of the foundation of the castle was the Tatar invasion in 1241-1242; due to the fear of another invasion, the castle was more strengthened. However, the Tatars could not completely attack targets on higher hills, people prefered to move close to the royal court. The majority of the new settlers were German imigrants. The second invasion of the Tatars were totally stopped by the troops of László Kun in 1285. At this time, the castle was already strengthened by consistent walls and towers, gates.

After the extinction of the Árpád-House (1301), Anjou Robert Carl won the dis-cordance around the royal court, became king and placed his throne in Visegrád, because previously Buda had supported his enemies. At the age of his son, Lajos the Great, the royal castle was set up in the south, and new civil settlement in the north.

The constructions, that were started by the Anjous, were continued by King Sigismund, and developed the most powerful castle in Europe by the first decade of the 15th century. The Royal Palace became a real royal center under the rule of King Sigismund (1387 – 1437) due to the construction of the „Fresh-Palace"; and reached its final expansion. The „Fresh-Palace" was finished in 1424, King Sigismund exhibited here the regalias brought to Buda. Sigismund was still alive, when the walls and the towers were set even more strong. Draw-

bridges, pitfalls of Wolves were set up. King Matthias (1458-1490) passed over the constructions, he put a lot of efforts on decorations, and the establishment of the renaissance culture, earning a widely known fame for the royal court. The gothic palace has been renewed in reneissance style. He strengthened the outer walls, the town faced a strong development. The golden age of the castle ended with the death of King Matthias. After the main defeat at Mohács

(1526), the Turks invaded the castle using a trick in 1541, and the age of the 150 year-old subjection started. The Turks only continued the development of the fortress, they did not pay attention on the conservation of the unnecessary buildings. During the siege of the United Christian Forces, the buildings were totally destroyed. In 1703, Buda became a Free Royal City. During the rule of the Habsburgs, the Castle District became significant again in the 18th century. In 1873, Pest, Buda and Óbuda united, and the new capital was formed, and an important development era came up.

During the Second World War, all buildings were destroyed, the Royal Palace burnt out. After the war, the Palace was rebuilt, and the buildings were renovated bit by bit. Due to the

natural beauty of the city, the Castle Hill is still the most remarkable piece of the cityscape.

The streets of the Castle Hill are the most liked walking areas of the people. A town from the Middle Ages, intimate little streets, old houses, street lamps, and wonderful art relics. The main street of the quarter starts from the Dísz square and goes towards the Matthias Church, named Tárnok street. The squares and the streets go along little colored houses. The winding streets and the narrow buildings are from the Middle age, sometimes there are valuable gothic windows and doors on these buildings. The elegant baroque palaces were built after the era of the Turks. The most interesting parts of the houses in the quarter are the housings. After the Turkish era, during the constructions they were walled, and were only found at the bombing of the district in the world war. Once the servants used to take a rest in the housings, decorated by roman, gothic and reneissance pieces. These housings are the unique pieces of the district, making Buda famous.

Besides several museums placed in the castle, (Hun-

garian National Gallery, Ludwig Museum, The Museum of Military History, Golden Eagle Pharmacy Museum, Hungarian Museum of Catering and Trade, Jewish Tabernacle from the Middle Age, Telephone Museum, Museum of Music) the National Széchenyi Library is also located here; several valuable collections and private galleries can be found in this quarter. The curiosity of the buildings is the basements: they were connected to each other due to Synagogue reasons, and were used during wartime. The defenders of the castle could use these basements to move troops from one place to another.

The Palace of the Buda Castle

The Ludwig Museum, the Hungarian National Gallery, the National Széchenyi Library and the Museum of Budapest is located here. The main gate is made out of wrought iron, a work of Gyula Jungfer. The Turul Hawk monument, set for the Millennium festivity, is the work of Gyula Donáth. The Ludwig Museum was officially opened in the June of 1991 in the „A" building of the palace. The new museum is founded

by the grants of Peter and Irene Ludwig: The art collector couple granted more than one hundred valuable pieces for Hungary; they can be seen at the permanent exhibition of the Museum, some contemporary

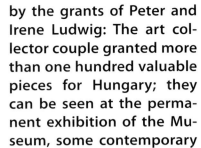

Hungarian works attached. Moved to the Palace of Arts in 2005. The Hungarian National Gallery was founded in 1957, and shows an overview of the art from the middle age up to date. The museum took possession of several collections even back from 1851. The eastern side of the palace building, facing the Danube, was designated for the museum. The exhibitions show the masterpieces of Hungarian Art.

National Széchenyi Library was placed in the National Museum before 1985. It was formed by the initiation of Ferenc Széchenyi, who granted 15000 books and 2000 writings to the Library. Nowadays the library has 5 million books. The most valuable treasuries are the first Hungarian writings from the 13th century, and the library of King Matthias, so called the Corvinas. This wing of the palace was designed by Miklós Ybl. There is an elevator from the palace to the Dózsa squre.

The Historical Museum of Budapest presents the history of the city from the ancient ages up to date. The most interesting attractions are the restored walls and towers and courts. In the palace, below the ground level, they restored the royal hall and the chapell into original shape.

The Square of the Holy Trinity

The major square of the Castle District, it used to be the city center in the Middle Age. Markets, processions, pageantries were often held here.The overview of the roomy square developed around 1700; it was naped of the main sculpture in the middle: the Holy Trinity. It was dedicated for the end of the plague pandemic between 1711 and 1714. The main composition is the work of Fülöp Ungleich of Eisenstadt, the embrossments were made by Antal Hörger.

The Matthias Church

The main church of the Castle named after Nagyboldogasszony, generally just called the Matthias Church, has its history closely connected to the history of the city of Buda. The first charter that mentions the church is dated in 1247, and places the church under the order of the bishop of Veszprém. Béla IV mentions the church as a one under construction and renovation. In 1269, the King released a charter, that introduces the church as a finished one, that can hold masses. Several political acts were taken among the walls of the church during the centuries. After the extinction of the Árpád-House, the principals greeted Wenceslas czech king here, who wanted to occupy the throne. In 1302, the people of Buda fulminated the Pope of Rome in the church. In 1309, Anjou Robert Carl was coronated here. After the coronation of King Matthias, the mess was celebrated here, and he held both of his weddings in this church. In the Middle Age, kings were coronated in the Basilica of Székesfehérvár, however, presented themselves for

the public in the Matthias Church for the first time. The church earned its shape and layout under the rule of King Sigismund. The bell-tower of the south-east was built under the rule of Matthias; the church has been named by the public after the coat of arms of Matthias: Matthias Church. In 1526, the Turks inva-ded Buda for a short period of time, but unfortunately the church partially burnt down. It had been renovated, but later in 1541, the Turks finally occupied the Castle, the church was turned to be a mosque, and was named: Eski-, or Bueyuek Dsamee, Large-, or Old Mosque. The Suliman Sultan held his Thanksgiving mess in the church. The inner furniture of the church was removed, the scupltures were taken away and the wall paintings were whitewashed. Two beautiful candelabras were taken away to Constantinaples, today both can be seen in the Haghia Sophia Mosque. The Christian troops invaded Buda on the 2nd of September 1686, and the Mosque turned to be the Church of Maria again. First the grey friars, later the Jesuists got the church; it was ren-

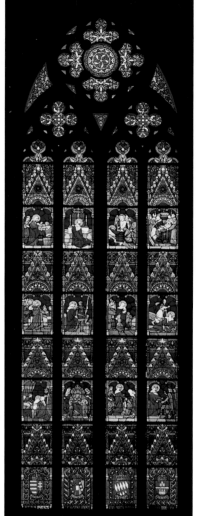

ovated again, and decorated in baroque style. In 1723, a combustion ruined the church; 25 years later, a lightning striked the building and damaged the main altar from 1690. By the end of the 19th century, the general condition of the church became so bad, that an overall renovation took place from 1873 to 1896 (planned by Frigyes Schulek). The exterior was rebuilt in the original neo-gothic style; on the wall paintings, the usual biblic scenes, and the major happenings of the Hungarian history can be seen. It has an outstanding acoustic ability, so sometimes concerts are held in the main nave.

The Fisherman's Bastion

The Fisherman's Bastion was built in 1905 on the site where the former fish-market took place. It never had a tactical reason, it has alwasy been used as an outlook; it was built to make the view of Pest more impressive. The highlighted bastions show a very picturesque view at night. This part of the city has been accepted as a part of the UNESCO World Heritage in 1988. At the feet of the bastions is a cemetery chapel of Saint Michael.

The Gellért Hill and Surroundings

The ascent Gellért Hill is a popular target of excursions in the city: 140 meters above the level of the Danube, there is a wonderful view of the whole city. On the southern side, there was an Eraviscus settlement before the age of Rome. Long ago it was called „Old Mountain", and had several superstitions. In a.d. 1046 AD, the polish born bishop (Saint) Gellért tried to evangelize pagans at this place; he was forced into a barrel and were threw down from the hillside. In the middle ages, people thought the place was used to witchcraft ceremonies. The Turks built a little fort on the top of the hill to control Buda better. After the fall of the freedom fight 1848-49, the Austrians built a Fortress – The Citadella – here to awe Hungarians.

The Statue of Liberty

The enormous statue on the top of the Gellért Hill is the artwork of an outstanding Hungarian sculptor, Zsigmond Kisfaludy Stróbl. The Memorial Staue was raised in 1947 for the rememberance of the Liberation of the country. The statue standing on the plinth is 14 meters high. The main figure of the statue is a woman holding a frond. There are two allegoric compositions below, they represent the progress and the fight against evil.

Statue of St. Gellért

The huge statue was set up in 1904 at the same place, where, the bishop died as a martyr in the 11th century. The saint holds a cross in his hand up high; an evangelized person kneels in front of him. The creator of this statue is Gyula Jankovics. The half-circled portico behind him was planned by Imre Francsek. The waterfall is fed by water from the fountain nearby.

Hotel Gellért and Spa

The Gellért Hill involves several fountains. The first comments on the fountains come from the 13th century, from the age of King Andrew II. The king built a hospital here to prevent black plague trusting the healing power of the water. In the age of the Turks, there was a thermal spa at this place. The healing power of the water was mentioned by the famous Turkish world-traveller Evlia Tshelebi. The hotel was built between 1912 and 1918 in modernist-secessionist style according to the

plans of Ármin Hegedűs, Artúr Sebestyén and Izidor Stark. The hotel has 300 beds and unites the functions of a luxury hotel and a spa. The healing water is used to treat rheuma, nervous-system disorders, digestion and joint problems. Besides the spa, the hotel has a swimming pool, whirlpool bath and wave-bath.

The Downtown and Surroundings

The downtown, or rather the foundation of the old Pest is dated back to the 11th century, it used to be a merchant settlement. In the middle age, Pest was a walled town with little villages nearby its scent borders. After the re-annexation, the villages were empty and their territories were attached to Pest. So the independent and suvereign town became the downtown. Its territory is basically constant and equals the area surrounded by high and strong walls built in the late 15th century. This wall from the age of Matthias was built with strong towers; those defended the gateways of the town. The middle age development culminated in the reign of Matthias in the 15th century. In the 17th century, Pest was in ruins and had just a few inhabitants. In the upcoming decades, new districts had been born, which became the suburbs of the city core. In 1838, a devastating flood destroyed Pest. Budapest was born in 1873 with the unification of Pest, Buda and Óbuda. After the settlements in the 19th century, huge public and private buildings were constructed with shops and cafes. At this time Pestbecame a centre of commerce and industry; the Liberty and Elizabeth Bridges were built, the Andrássy Avenue and the most exclusive street of the city, former Lipót, now called Váci street.

The Vigadó

The construction of the Vigadó was finished in 1833 by the plans of Mihály Pollack. The first senate held its seats here during the freedom fight of 1848-49. Due to heavy cannonade, the building caught fire and burnt down. Today's Vigadó was built in the place of the former one by the plans of Frigyes Feszl in classicist style between 1859 and 1864. The front of the Vigadó is decorated with traditional motifs, kings, rulers, and the sculptures of other principals. In the main stairway, the paintings of Károly Lotz and Mór Than can be seen.

The Hungarian Academy of Science

Engineered by a Berliner, the eclectic-neo-renaissance palace was built by the plans of Friedrich August Stühler between 1862 and 1864. The front decoration of the two floored building was made by E. Wolf and Miklós Izsó. The inside of the Academy has also a very fancy decoration. Its scientific library is one of the most significant libraries in Hungary.

The Gresham Palace

The palace used to be the Budapest center of the London-based Gresham Insurance Company. It was built in secessionist style in 1907 with remarkable beauty, wonderful front side topped with sculptures. Planners were the Vágó brothers and Sigmund Quittner. The modernity of the Gresham Palace became the pride of Budapest. In this building, several brand new technical „wonders" were used for exaple the centralised vacuum cleaners. In the cafe on the mezziane floor, young artists used to meet each other, later became the Gresham-Table. After renovation, it operates as a hotel.

Vörösmarty Squares

Ancient traffic crossing, the main gateway to Vác stood nearby long ago. It was named from its Vörösmarty statue in 1919. The brass statue stands on a plinth made of white marble, was augurated in 1865 and it is the artwork of Miklós Vay. Originally it had been placed in the middle of the square facing downtown, but was removed to its new place due to heavy traffic. Other sights of the square is a fount decorated with lions and a large drinking fountain. On the side of the square, there is the Gerbeaud confectionery, which is internationally known of its products and role in the public life. The square is the starting point of the Millennium Underground towards the City Park.

The Parliament

The largest and most known building in Hungary, the symbol of Budapest. The imposing building was built between 1885 and 1902 according to the plans of Imre Steindl; he died several weeks before the ribbon cutting ceremony. The first seat of the Parliament took place here in the year of the Millennium, on the 8th of June 1896. The influence of the Parliament of London (by Charles Barry) can be seen on the building. The fronts of this eclectic building are ne-ogothic, while it has a renaissance nad baroque layout. The building is divided into three parts: the major and center part is the dome; on the two sides the floor of the Parliament and the floor of

the congress can be found, formerly the house of the Lords and the Senate. The lenght of the parliament is 268 metres, the width is 118 meters. The height is 96 meters, layout is 17.745 m2 and has 691 rooms. The length of the stairs is about 20 kilometers. The outside of the building is decorated with 88 sculptures; besides the seven leaders, rulers, counts of Transsylvania, generals and brave men are formed. The main front faces

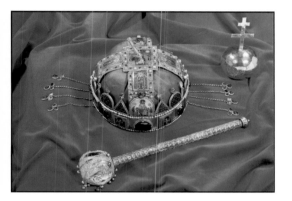

the Danube, where the Parliament is decorated with huge arches. The main entrace is from the Kossuth Square; the two lions were designed by Béla Markup. The main stairway, with sculptures, paintings, leads us to the 21 meter diameter wide, 27 meters high, polygon dome. The symbols of the state, the Saint Crown, the Orb and the Sceptre is located here; they can be visited by organised trips.

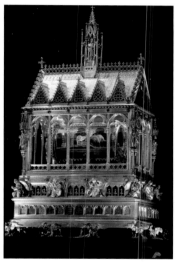

St. Stephen's Basilica

The largest church of the city with the capacity of 8500 seats. The dome is 96 meters high, just like the Parliament. The construction started in 1851; after the death of the architect József Hild, Miklós Ybl continued to work on the building. Supervising the plans, he discovered that there were statical mistakes in it. Soon after in the January 1868, the walls have collapsed due to the sag of the main pilons. The only

EGO SUM VIA VERITAS ET VITA

eye witness was Miklós Ybl, although the collapse happened daytime. Ybl had made new plans and the construction went on. Due to the death of Ybl, the church was finished by József

Kauser in 1906; the best atrists of that age were involved in the inner decoration. The basilica was built in neoreneissance style, the facade faces the Danube. The diameter of the dome is 22 meters. In the right side tower, the largest bell of Hungary can be found, weighting 9 tonns.

The dome rules the three naves; the main altar is in the apsis of the sanctum. Behind the main altar, there is the sculpture of Saint Stephen, who is the patron saint of the church. Created by Alajos Stróbl. On the 900th anniversary of the death of Saint Stephen in 1938, the Basilica earned the Basilica Minor rank. The main treasure of the Basilica snd the most valuable relic of the Hungarian Catholic Church is the mummified right hand of St. Stephen that can be found in the chapel at the rear of the church behind the altar.

44

The Museum of Handicrafts

The Museum of Handicrafts of Budapest was formed after the institutions of London and Vienna, third in Europe. The museum was opened by emperor Francis Joseph in 1896, in a wonderful secessist building planned by Ödön Lechner and Gyula Pártos. Lechner used Zsolnay china for the decorations of the roof. The building was constructed according to the most modern museum-building theories. The inner space is one big exhibition hall with many exhibition rooms. The importance of the building in the mainsteam of international secession is an unquestionable fact, however many arguments were around about the building. The collection was founded in 1872, having pieces of handicrafts.

The Central Shopping Hall

At the end of the 19th century, five big volume shopping halls were built in Budapest, in a very similar style. They were opened on the same day. The Central Shopping Hall was planned by Samu Petz, the professor of the Technical University of Budapest. This is the largest: the main building is 150 meters long, and six naves join from each side. The main attraction is the roofing. Back in those days, the lighting, the roofing, the refrigerated chambers were all very modern. The large basement were filled with foodstuff even from ships. The hall, opened in 1897, has been renovated recently.

The Synagogue

The biggest synagogue of Europe; built between 1854 and 1859, designed by Ludwig Förster, an architect of Vienna, in a Bisantic-Moor style. It differs from synagogues in general, the size and the interior is similar to a roman catholic church. The towers near the facade has a church-like impression. The main attraction of the facade is the huge rose-window. The synagogue has 3 naves, and according to the orthodox traditions, separated balcony was built for the women. 3000 believers can be seated. There are several valuable appointments, especially the works of Frigyes Feszl and Áron Hakodesz. In 1931, László Vágó built a new nave to the Wesselényi street-side, and placed the most valuable jewish collection in it – hadicrafts from the Roman Empire, old printed books...etc. The most valuable piece is the book of Chevra Kashida from 1792. The archway around the church became a cemetery in 1944-45, where the victims of the nazism were buried.

The State Opera House

The neo-renaissance style Hungarian State Opera, opened on 27th of September 1884, looks like the major imposing opera houses throughout Europe. The building is the major work of Miklós Ybl. The richly articulated facade is decorated by arches, pillars, and sculptures. In the two housings at the driveway, the sculptures of the two greatest Hungarian composers can be found: Ferenc Erkel and Ferenc Liszt. In the other housings of the facade, there are four sculptures of the muses: Erato (amorous literature) Therpsikhore (dance), Thalia (comedy) and Melphomene (tragedy). There are two Sfinxes on the side of the building made out of marble from Carrara. Inside the building, there are several masterworks of Alajos Stróbl, Károly Lotz, but also the paintings of Bertalan Székely, Mór Than, Mihály Kovács can be seen. The U-shaped auditorium is one of the most beautiful in Europe, has great acoustic parameters, and 1200 people can be seated.

The Hungarian National Museum

The museum is open from 1802, and thanks its existence for Ferenc Széchenyi, who dedicated his collection of coins, books, and writings to the Nation. The classicist building was designed by Mihály Pollack, was built between 1837 and 1847; one of the most beautiful building of that era. The museum occupies a 109 x 70 meter rectangle, with two inner courts. The sill-height is 24 meters, the built-in surface is 7894 m2. The sculptures of the tympan are the works of Milano's Raffael Monti: in the centre seats Pannonia with two laureates handing them to the impersonators of science and arts on the right, and history and fame on the left. The sculpture in the right corner represents the Danube, in the left corner the Drava. The inner structure of the building represents the classicist design. The walls and the ceiling of the main stairway are decorated by the allegoric paintings of Károly Lotz and Mór Than. The museum played an important role in the 1848-49 Hungarian Revolution and War of Independence. In the garden of the museum, many famous Hungarian writers, scientists, artists have their own memorials. Facing the main entrace, there is the monument of the poet János Arany made out of brass and chalk, raised in 1893. The museum has a rich collection, visiting it shows the rough history of Hungary.

The Duna river

The Margareth Island

Maybe the nicest park of Budapest. The history leads us back to the ancient Roman ages. The borderlines of Pannonia Provence involved the islands too; the original name of the island was Insula Leporum (found in a 13th century charter), the Island of the Rabbits. For a long time, it used to be the place for religious withdrawals, it was hard to reach in the middle of the Danube. The major art relics of the island are the ruins of a monastic church, and the ruins of a nunnery where Margareth, the daughter of Béla the Fourth, was living, and whom after the island was named. Béla the Fourth vowed to God, upon he can stop the invasion of the Tatars in 1241, he offers his daughter for God, and schools her for him. He kept his promise, so the church and the nunnery was built, where the nine-year-old Margareth was sent in 1251. Margareth lived an austeric life and died in the age of 29. The island was opened for the public in 1869, and a horse tramway was put into service on it. Prior to the construction of the Margareth bridge, the island could had been reached only by boat. The bridge was finished in 1876, the side-bridge was opened in 1900. From this point, the island became a touristic attraction.

The Bridges

The Danube had an important role in history, it crosses the city, divides Buda and Pest. The river reaches the border line of Budapest at the Southern tip of the Szentendre-island. Along the banks of the river, there are every sights that means the essence of Budapest. Several bridges links the two sides; those bridges crossing the river are not just for the city sight, but also artistic pieces itselves. During the second world war, nazi troops blew every single bridge up.

The Margareth bridge was projected by a French engineer Ernest Gouin. The river piers are assymetric, the two branches of the Danube joins each other here after the Margareth Island. The bridge was under construction from 1872-1876; a side-bridge was attached to the Margareth Island in 1899-1900. The sculptures on the river piers are the work of Frenchman Adolphe Thabart.

The Chain-Bridge was constructed between 1839 and 1849 by the initiation of István Széchenyi. Planned by the Englisman William Tierney Clark, and carried out by Adam Clark (not relatives). The bridge is 380 meters long, and the suspension of the bridge on the two river piers was a technical wonder back in

that age. The heads of the bridge are guarded by huge stone lions, the works of János Marschalkó. According to the tales, the lions do not have tongues; when they figured this out, the sculptor jumped into the Danube. In reality, the lions have tongues, but cannot be seen.

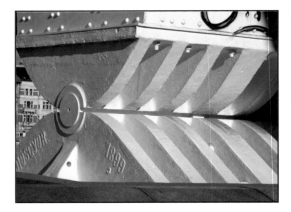

Elisabeth-bridge: todays bridge was built between 1961 and 1964; the old bridge has been totally destroyed in the second world war; projected by Pál Sávoly. The first Elisabeth-bridge was constructed between 1897 and 1903. It was a single span bridge, back in those days, the largest on the world. Despite the old bridge was decorated with secessionist pieces, the new one is a minimalist, simple cable-bridge.

The Freedom Bridge was constructed between 1894 and 1899; designed by János Feketeházy; named before: Bridge of Vámház Square, later Francis Joseph Bridge. The bridge was renamed after reconstruction in 1946. All of the old decorating pieces have been restaurated, the turul-hawks and the royal coat of arms still can be seen.

The City Woods (Városliget)

The biggest park of Budapest. This swampy area used to be the hunting ground of the King. Emperor Lipót awarded the territory to the city. Under the rule of Maria Theresia, the swamp was drained, trees were planted. In the 19th century, an English style park was built here. Famous in history, all facilities of the Millennium was placed here in 1896. This festivity was held for the foundation of the Hungarian State 1000 years ago. In these new built facilities, the culture of Hungary, the landscapes, the cities, the industry, the trade and the agriculture was represented. For this occasion, the first underground of the European Continent was put into service. In this era, the Musaum of Fine Arts, the Heroes' Square and the Vajdahunyad castle was built nearby.

The Heroes' Square

This is the most representative square of Budapest. The Millenium Festivity was opened here, and the artwork of György Zala and Albert Schikedanz was raised: the Millennium Memorial, that represents the patriot feelings of the Hungarians. In the portico, sculptures of famous Hungarian Kings and Principals are placed. Gabriel archangel stands on the top of the major post; with the Holy Crown in his right hand, and with the apostolic double cross in his left. According to the legend, Gabriel apprared in the dreams of Saint Stephen and brought him the crown. On the plinth of the major post, there are the legendary seven leaders of the Hungarians, who occupied the Carpathian basin. The whole Monument was completely finished in 1929. Most of the sculptures are the work of György Zala. Right from the monument, there is the art gallery for contemporary arts and handcrafts. Left from it, there is the Museum of Fine Arts. The two buildings are not the same. The Museum of Fine Arts is larger, but placed more in the back from the monument so it balances the difference of those two buildings on the square.

The Museum of Fine Arts

The building, closing the square from the left, was finished in 1906. In the tymphan, right above the main entrace, are the copy of the Zeus sculptures from Olympia, Greece: The Dance of the Centaurs and Laphites. Overviewing the building, the reneissance is the major style. The museum is rich in egyptian, greek, roman, spanish collections, and usually hosts foreign exhibitions too.

The Art Gallery

The eclectic building was built in 1895. It's layout and front decorations showns a reneissance view. The decorations were made „antifreeze" pyrogranite. The tymphan was decorated in 1941; it used to operate as a war hospital during WW I. It was completely renovated between 1992 and 1994 in original shape. This building became the most modern and beautiful art gallery of Europe.

The Vajdahunyad Castle

Probably the most interesting group of buildings of the Városliget (city Park). Originally built for the Millenium Exhibition from wood and cardboard to represent our architectural past. The task of the designer was to present all the historicalstyles of architecture to be found in Hungary on the basis of existing buildings but ensure that the whole building should give a homogeneous impression. The complex of historical buildings had such success, that later on the building was built permanently with stone. The design incorporates the most beautiful Hungarian architectural elements. We can find here the exact copy of the gate of Ják Chapel, representing the XIII th century Roman era. The originals of the towers and bastions can be found in Transylvania, they are the gems of Vajdahunyad Castle. Gothic, Renaissance and Baroque elements can also be detected in the building. Through a stone bridge we reach the courtyard, which houses the Museum Of Agriculture.. Here we can admire the statue of Anonymus, who was thought to have been the notary of King Béla III. The statue is the work of Ligeti Miklós and was erected in 1903.

The Zoo

The zoo was founded by the initiation of János Xantus; who was a lawyer, biologist, ethnogarphist. Originally it was founded by a private company in 1865. In the first years there were only animals, later plant houses were built in 1872. At the beginning of the 20th century, the zoo announced bankruptcy, and in 1907, the city bought the institution. In this age, the house of the animals were raised and the main gate decorated with elephants. The zoo tries to provide natural living conditions for the animals.